For travelers

—*M. H.*

For Clay

—*R. J. W.*

Text copyright © 2002 by Margaret Hodges
Illustrations copyright © 2002 by Richard Jesse Watson

Published 2002 by Eerdmans Books for Young Readers
An imprint of Wm. B. Eerdmans Publishing Company
255 Jefferson SE, Grand Rapids, Michigan 49503
P.O. Box 163, Cambridge CB39PU U.K.
All rights reserved.
Printed and bound in Hong Kong

02 03 04 05 06 07 08   7 6 5 4 3 2 1

Library of Congress Cataloging-in-Publication Data
Hodges, Margaret, 1911-
The Legend of Saint Christopher / written by Margaret Hodges; illustrated by Richard Jesse Watson
p. cm.
Summary: Relates the story of Offero, whose service to Jesus brought him the name of
Christopher the Christ-bearer and caused him to be called the patron saint of travelers.
ISBN 0-8028-5077-4 (alk. paper)
1. Christopher, Saint—Juvenile literature. [1. Christopher, Saint. 2. Saints.]
I. Watson, Richard Jesse, ill. II. Title.

BR1720.C485 H63 2002
270.1'092—dc21
2002021613

The illustrations were painted in oils on abstract acrylic backgrounds.
The book title was hand lettered by John Stevens.
The text type was set in Cochin.

The Legend of SAINT CHRISTOPHER

The Legend of SAINT CHRISTOPHER

from *The Golden Legend*
Englished by William Caxton, 1483

Adapted by Margaret Hodges
Illustrated by Richard Jesse Watson

Eerdmans Books for Young Readers
Grand Rapids • Cambridge, U.K.

Foreword

This is the story of a man who was called a saint, and later, the patron saint of travelers, especially at Christmastime. It was first written in the thirteenth century *Golden Legend,* a collection of wonder tales compiled by Jacobus de Voragine. The stories were arranged by seasons of the year and were not meant to be historical. The original authors may have been schoolboys in monastery schools.

In days of old, there lived a man called Offero. His name meant "The Bearer."

He was very tall and strong, and his face was fierce and bold. He served the king of the land where he lived. But he wanted to find an even greater king. He wanted to find the greatest king in the world — to serve him as his bearer.

So Offero went out and searched until he found a king who some said was the greatest in the world. And Offero served in his court.

One day a minstrel came to the court and sang a song about the devil. Trembling, the king made the sign of a cross as he listened to the song. Offero was amazed and wondered what the sign meant.

At first the king would not tell him. But Offero said, "Tell me what the sign means, or I shall leave your court."

So the king told him, "When I hear the devil's name and make the sign of the cross, the devil cannot harm me."

Offero said, "You fear the devil? That means the devil is mightier than you. I thought I had found the mightiest and the greatest lord in all the world, but I was wrong. Farewell — I will go to find the devil and be his servant."

So Offero left the king and went to find the devil. As he went through a great desert he saw a knight with a cruel face half hidden by his armor.

"Where are you going?" asked the knight.

"I am looking for the devil," said Offero. "I want him for my master, because he is stronger than the greatest king in the world."

"I am the one you seek," said the knight. "I am the devil."

Then Offero swore to be the devil's servant and took him for his master.

As they went along together, they saw a cross standing by the side of the road. When the devil saw the cross, he was afraid and fled.

Offero was amazed. He ran after the devil and asked why he had run away. But the devil would not tell him.

Offero said, "If you will not tell me, I will leave you and serve you no more."

The devil was forced to answer since he wanted Offero to serve him. "There was a man called Christ who died on a cross. When I see his sign, I am afraid."

"Since you flee from his sign, he must be greater and mightier than you," said Offero. "I have made a mistake. I have not found the greatest lord of the world. I will serve you no longer, and I will go to look for Christ."

Offero searched for a long time to find Christ. At last he came to a lonely place where a hermit lived. Offero asked the hermit where he could find Christ.

The hermit answered, "If you would find him, go and live by yonder river. The river is deep and wide, and many people have drowned when they tried to cross. You are tall and strong. If you live by the river, you can carry people over. Our Lord Jesus Christ will be pleased to see you helping travelers, and I hope he will show himself to you."

Offero replied, "I can do this service, and I promise that I will."

He went to the river's edge and built himself a hut. When anyone came to cross the river, Offero took a great staff in his hand to guide his steps. Then he carried the person on his shoulders through the deep water to the other side.

For many days Offero lived at the river's edge. Winter came, and snow lay deep on the ground. One cold and windy night, as Offero slept in his hut, he heard the voice of a child calling him.

"Offero — Offero — come out and carry me over the river."

Offero rose and went out, but he saw no one. He went into his hut again. Then once more he heard the voice crying, "Offero — Offero — come out and bear me over."

But he ran out and found nobody.

A third time he was called, and when he ran out he saw a child standing by the brink of the river.

"Will you carry me safely over the water?" asked the child.

"I will carry you," Offero answered.

Then he lifted the child onto his shoulders. He took his staff in his hand and stepped down into the river. The water was icy cold. It rose higher and higher around him. The child was as heavy as lead on his shoulders, and as Offero went farther, the water swirled wildly about them. The child grew heavier and heavier, and Offero feared they would drown.

At last he struggled out of the deep water and felt the ground firm beneath his feet. When he came to the far side of the river he set the child down and said, "Child, you have put me in great danger. You were so heavy that I felt as if I had all the world on my shoulders. I did not know that I could carry such a load."

And the child answered, "When you carried me on your shoulders, you carried the world, for I have the whole world in my hands. I am Jesus Christ, the King whom you serve. And you will no longer be called Offero — but Christopher, the Christ-bearer. When you are gone, others will come, remembering you and helping travelers on their way. So that you will know I say the truth, set your staff in the earth by your door. Tomorrow it will bear flowers and fruit."

As the child spoke, he vanished.

Christopher turned and made his way back across the river. That night he set his staff in the earth by the door of his little hut. And when he rose in the morning, he found that his staff had taken root in the earth. It was covered with leaves and fruit and bright flowers blooming in the snow.

For the rest of his life, the face of Christopher was joyful and youthful like that of a child. And in memory of him, travelers to this day carry pictures of him to help them on their journeys.

Comes again the blessed Christmas.

Christ, a little Child,

Finds the river flowing ever

Deep and dark and wild.

May I help a weary traveler

On his journey go.

See the staff beside my doorway

Blossoming in snow.

— M. H.